AF413469

The Blue House Across the Street

The Blue House Across the Street

Observations On Life from Outside the Puppy Mill

Sally Kersch

Sally's Mom

IngramSpark

CONTENTS

CONTENTS

CONTENTS

This book is dedicated to all the rescue pups and the owners who rescued them.

My Fur-Ever Home

In my New House Across the Street from the Blue House Across the Street, I'm living in my fur-ever home. I have a mom that I love. I also have a brother that I love but I bark at him whenever he comes to see my mom. Only I can have Mom (HA!). There are 3 cats and a bunch of chickens. The chicken poop is delicious but Mom yells at me when I eat it. Oops.

I am fascinated by the Blue House Across the Street. I will keep an eye on that house. I hear dogs barking but never see them. The people that live there are the Parking Police. I don't know what that means but my mom says so, so it must be true.

End of Chapter 1. I need a nap.

The Escape

Mom finally got out of bed. I had to bark and growl at her. She doesn't seem to like mornings, but needed to go pottie!

Except I forgot to go pottie. A few nights ago I found a secret hole that goes under Mom's porch and leads to the place where we go for a walk and I got to run without my harness and leash! That was fun! Until The Man in the Brick House Next Door tricked me. Scooped me up and brought me back home. Mom was so happy I was found but scolded me at the same time. I wagged my tail and got lots of snuggles.

So now whenever I go outside Mom watches my every move. I run around like I'm looking for the perfect spot to pee but I'm really looking for me secret hole. I must get out! Mom has put up new obstacles everywhere to keep me safe. I sit and stare at the hole under the porch.

Now we are on the porch for Morning Coffee. I don't know what that means but mom is in a much better mood now. It's very quiet at The Blue House across the Street. I heard the dogs barking. I bet they have to go pottie too.

No Blue House Across the Street

All the windows are closed today. My Mom turned the heat back on. I don't know what that means but all the cats are snuggling with me. Mom's bed is toasty warm and my mom is happy we all slept in, whatever that means. Also no porch time, so I didn't see The Blue House Across the Street. I hope those pups got to go pottie. Mom says it's cold outside. The white rain is falling again. I got scolded because my paws are muddy. Duh Mom.

The Cat Named Harvie is crying. Mom says he's very sick. My brother came over and is very sad about The Cat Named Harvie. We all were very gentle with him. Harvie is my brother and I love him. I'm doing my best to be a good dog. It's a sad day at My New House Across the Street from The Blue House Across the Street.

The Haircut

This week was very long. My mom stayed home from work Monday because my brother, The Cat Named Harvie, died. Mom was very sad. My brother Ben came over too and wrapped him up safe so mom could take him to the vet to be cremated. I'm not sure what that means but a few days later he came back in a pretty little box. Mom put him on the mantle next to a candle. We miss him.

Mom works all week and I don't like that. I sleep on the

couch all day. I know she spies on me during the day because there is a camera that turns blue when she is watching. I go a bit crazy when she comes home. She calls me a silly pup but I don't care. I love my mom.

Saturday I got a haircut and got to see The Blue House Across the Street. My mom has a table with all sorts of brushes and scissors and clippers to make me look good. It's hard being still, but I did get to watch the neighborhood. This event took 2 DAYS! That's a lot for a pup like me. She says I was a good girl and got a pig ear for a treat. Then she noticed she missed a few spots. No more haircuts for me. I need a nap.

A Walk Around the Block

It's a good day at My New House Across the Street from the Blue House Across the Street! Mom is teaching me how to walk on a leash. She says I've got a lot to learn about being a good dog on a walk. BUT THERE ARE SO MANY SMELLS! I'm getting better though. I walk along the edge of the sidewalk and try not to make too many sudden moves and trip her. The Dog Named Lucy did that once and Mom fell and broke her arm. Oops.

When we got back to our house we saw the Parking Police at the Blue House Across the Street. He didn't say hi. Haven't heard the dogs barking either. Someone is making loud banging sounds in the neighborhood. Mom is annoyed.

A Shitty Day

My mom had a Shitty Day. Literally. We went for a walk and I pooped right on the sidewalk. No big deal says Mom until the poop bag splits and she gets my poop on her hand. Mom is mad, but not at me. I'm a good girl. The Dollar Tree poop bags are shitty...ha!

My mom had a friend over tonight. They laughed and ate

pizza. It was fun giving a stranger the stare down! Later on when my mom's friend called an Uber to take her home, the Parking Police at The Blue House Across the Street yelled at the Uber Man for being parked in front of his house. For like a minute. Let me say this...don't ever make my mom mad. She walked across the street and confronted the man. It was not good. In Texas you can get shot for this. I'm glad we don't live in Texas...whatever that means. My Mom is a bad ass and I lover her.

7

Hump Day

Finally a warm day to stare at The Blue House Across the Street. Mom thinks The Blue House Across the Street keeps an eye on My New House Across the Street (that's where I live). She thinks they have a camera aimed at their parking spot that I mentioned in Chapter 6. Parking Police always know when someone is in front of their house.

Mom says it's Hump Day and she's happy. Is she crazy? I grew up in a Puppy Mill and Hump Day was never a good day. I'm pretty traumatized at that phrase! I must chase the cats and chew up the mail to get back at her. I bet this chaos means I get treats!! But if I act too crazy she puts on my Thundershirt, which for some reason calms me down and takes all the craziness away. Then Mom is calm too. Either way, let's not mention Hump Day again. Time for a nap.

8

Oops

9

Vacation

    I finally met my Aunt Peggy. She was nice and talked very quietly to me. Gave me a couple of head scratches. Then her and Mom left the house for a while and when they came back I didn't like Aunt Peggy anymore (HA!). I gave lots of barks. Mom gave me lots of yells. Woof.

Sunday Mom and Aunt Peggy left for a million years. They called it vacation but I called it torture. My brother Ben and his friend Max came to see me and gave me treats and food. I barked at them.

After a million years (Mom said it was only three days), Mom and Aunt Peggy came home. I was sooo happy to see my mom that I hardly barked at Aunt Peggy. She jumps when I bark so sometimes I bark at her just to let her know who's boss. BARK!

It's just me and Mom now. The Cat Named Poe escaped this morning and Mom didn't even yell at him. How unfair is that? He came back on his own at supper time. Mom said he was a brat. I need to find out how he gets away with escapes and I don't. Maybe I'll stop chasing him and he'll tell me the secret. Time to stare at The Blue House Across the Street and ponder on all these life's mysteries...acceptable escapes and vacations. Woof.

The Fence

Mom is finally home from Work. I missed her. Work is like Vacation only she's gone for a 1000 years instead of a million. We did sit on the porch when she was home for lunch. Lots of noise at The Blue House Across the Street. Some men with big trucks and loud machines were installing what Mom called an Ugly Chain Link Fence around The Blue House Across the Street.

I'm happy for the fence. The three dogs that live there will get to run and play just like me! Maybe they will find an escape hole like I did and they can run to my house and we can be friends!

In other news Mom introduced me to Patio Living. All day Saturday Mom cleaned up "the mess" on the patio. I love the leaf blower! It's noisy but the wind is fun. Then Mom sat on the patio for a long time and listened to music. I even get my own chair! My brother Ben and my friend Max came over Sunday night and they cooked their food on The Grill. I only barked a little and when nobody was looking I stole the paper The Steak was wrapped in. It was delicious! But then Mom saw me and I got yelled at and got put back in the house. I was mad and I peed on the floor. Oops. Time for window watching...but first I have to growl at Fat Cat to get out of my spot.

11

It's A Dogs Life

I just realized after 10 chapters that I haven't said much about where I came from. My past wasn't fun. I lived in Missouri at a Puppy Mill. Puppies sound fun but not for the moms and dads, see Chapter 7. I lived in a cage and ate bad food. I had lots of puppies that I loved but didn't get to keep. My teeth were bad and fell out. It was a sad place.

Since living in My New House Across the Street from the Blue House Across the Street I'm living A Dog's Life. I had more teeth pulled but now I have yummy food to eat and my remaining teeth are pearly white. Mom gives me kibble with Parmesan cheese in the morning and kibble with warm beef broth for dinner. I have soft places to sleep and green grass to pee in...sometimes...oops. I have Cat Friends and Chicken Friends, a Brother and a Sister and Aunt Peggy, but mostly I have My Mom. I get special treats in puzzles to make me think and pig ears because I'm a good girl. I have a big back yard where I can do zoomies and don't get yelled at for trampling The Hostas...whatever that means.

I hardly remember life before My Mom. I still get a bit crazy but Mom calms me down with The Thundershirt. I still do bad things but only get scolded a little, followed by lots of hugs and kisses. I have morning coffee with Mom and get to look out the window...and let's not forget Patio Living, see Chapter 10. Mom likes to say that Life is Good and I couldn't agree more. If you ever get a chance for My Mom to be Your Mom, you will have the best life ever.

I'm going to give my mom lots of kisses now...Woof.

The Gnats

My Publisher pointed out to me that I skipped Chapter 8. I'm a dog. Oops.

In other news Mom keeps talking about The Gnats. When we are outside for Patio Living she goes crazy flaying her hands and itching almost as much as I do. She hates The

Gnats and although I don't know what they are I do know that they are interfering with my Patio Living. A friend of hers said their season will end in June. What is June? I have so much to learn...

The Blue House Across the Street has their air conditioner on. Mom says it's hot but with a low humidity and dew point. It was always hot in Missouri. I don't mind the heat now that I don't live in a crate. Looking across the street with a breeze in my face is heaven.

Time to pretend I have to go pottie so I can go outside. Maybe Mom will come out with me and be brave against The Gnats.

Chipmunks, Snuggles and Ritz Crackers

My newest obsession is the Chipmunks. They are smaller than the Squirrels but just as fast. They don't climb the tree or the fence though. They are very sneaky and hide under the siding on Mom's Garage or behind the fence where I've smashed all The Hostas. Oops. I can smell them and hear them but they are very fast. Mom doesn't like them because they eat her tomatoes and steal treats from the chickens. I'm trying hard to catch them for Mom. I bet she'll be so proud of me!

I've also discovered how warm and comfy Mom's lap is. I mean, I've sat on her lap before. But the snuggles I'm getting are the best. I even get snuggles when she is sewing! I love my mom.

Mom has been giving me bits of People Food. One day I got to lick her breakfast plate. Eggs are delicious! I will not chase the chickens anymore. Last night she gave me a Ritz Cracker. Buttery Goodness! Mom say's everything tastes better when it's sittin' on a Ritz!

I haven't seen the Parking Police at the Blue House Across the Street this week. Mom says maybe they went on vacation. I don't like vacation because Mom leaves for a million years. I hope the dogs are ok. A million years is a long time and they will be lonely. My friends who live in The Brick House Next Door are watering their plants. I watch them every night. Neighbors are a good thing (unless you park in front of their house).

I'm going to sit on my chair and guard the yard. Maybe I will get more Ritz Crackers if I catch the Chipmunks. Wish me luck.

14

I'm in Big Trouble

Not a good week at My New House Across the Street from the Blue House Across the Street. Mom says I've been a Bad Dog...

Peed and pooped in the house...completely missing the pee pads. Peed on Mom's clothes. Oops.

I've also been working very hard to dig my way out of the backyard under the fence. Smashed a plant. I did make several successful escapes which all landed me in Big Trouble. Mom gets mad when I don't come when she calls my name. I have very selective hearing. Saturday a man named Steve came and fixed the fence. Filled in my holes and everything! Now I can't get out under the porch or through the neighbors fence. I will continue to seek escape!

I saw the The Man who lives at the Blue House Across the Street cutting his grass today. He takes a very long time doing this. He loves his yard. Mom could take a few pointers from him.

This week is a Holiday with loud noises. It's called the 4th of July. I don't like this Holiday. I get very scared and hide and Mom can't find me. Then I pee on her clothes. I will be a very happy and Good Dog when this Holiday is over. Time to hide.

SALLY KERSCH

15 █

Caturday

I don't always sit and stare at The Blue House Across the Street. Sometimes I sit on Mom's Lap. Sometimes I lay on the Tuffet, whatever that is. Sometimes I sit on my Mom's blanket and eat my treat.

Sometimes The Cats take over my bed. I guess that's ok. They take lots of naps, watch the birds and do a cat version of a growl when stray cats wander buy. Mom thinks that's funny.

The breeze that comes through the window is relaxing. The noise from the cars is soothing. Unless it's a motorcycle. That's annoying.

It's important to have comfy places to nap. We all love to sit near Mom and sleep. Mom makes everything better.

I hope Mom takes a nap today.

A Week in Review

Monday was a good day! Mom stayed home with me. She did lots of lawn work. I didn't like that she was outside without me (she says I can't be trusted in the front yard without a leash) but she took lots of breaks and I got lots of cuddles. After that she went into some sort of cleaning frenzy and cleaned the Side Porch. I got yelled at because she found my poop out there...oops. It looks really nice out there now.

A big comfy couch Mom calls The Davenport is out there. Mom says it's the perfect spot for naps. I love naps almost as much as Mom.

The squirrels have invaded our yard and are driving me crazy. Mom says it's because the walnut tree on the other side of the fence is loaded with treats the squirrels love. I sit and stare at the tree in our backyard. They taunt me running up and down that tree. I try to climb it but all I managed to do is smash Mom's Hostas...oops.

My Brother Ben came over and I barked at him. Then I sniffed his hand and gave him a kiss. That made him happy. I bark at him because he needs to know who's boss. He just laughs and pats me on my head.

Mom bought me a dress. That woman is crazy. Do I look like a pink dress kind of pup? It made Mom smile so I put up with the dress.

Now it's Sunday. Mom can't go anywhere because her alternator died. I don't know what that means but she is worried about getting it to Car Fix-It Man. I'm sitting in my window-watching spot keeping an eye on The Blue House Across the Street and guarding my pig ear from the cats. Mom is drinking her coffee. Porch Living is the best. I have the best life...except for that pink dress...

17

Where in the World is Sally Kersch?

What a crazy two weeks. Mom worked a million days in a row, made me wear diapers and The Cats have taken over my bed where I watch The Blue House Across the Street. I am not a happy pup.

First, the diapers. How humiliating. I guess Mom had enough of me peeing on the floor. The joke was on her though...the diapers didn't stop me from pooping on the floor! One day I wrestled my diaper off and it smelled up her side of the bed. Big mistake on my part. Lots of yells and no cuddles. Guess she really is the boss of me...I better shape up.

Squirrel Watching is in high gear right now. Lots of nuts falling from the tree in the Apartment House next to our house. I sit outside for hours, just waiting for the right moment to chase The Squirrels. Haven't caught one yet but I'm not giving up.

Now for The Cats. I don't know why they have taken over my spot. They have what Mom calls a Cat Tree where they nap and stare at The Blue House Across the Street. It has a way better view. I think it's my Snoopy bed they like. Who doesn't love Snoopy?

Mom buried a chicken today. She felt bad for her Happy

Hen and buried her under the tree in the front yard. She didn't let me help. I'm a good digger! See Chapter 14. Also, I'm not allowed in the front yard...Mom says I can't be trusted unless I have my leash on. Woof, Mom...just woof.

18

International Dog Day

Happy Dog Day! May your day be filled with treats, pets, long walks and afternoons chasing rabbits!

Guess what???!!!??? I CAUGHT A RABBIT!! I CAUGHT A RABBIT!! IT WAS DELICIOUS!! I AM A FIERCE HUNTING DOG!!

What a fun morning of hunting! I figured out that if I

cause enough chaos in the morning before the Alarm Clock goes off, Mom will let me outside early for my morning "pottie time". Who are we kidding here, Mom. We all know that I go pottie inside and purposely only pee on a corner of the pee pad.

Oops...where was I? Rabbit Hunting! Anyway, Mom went back to bed to wake up some more. She is NOT a morning person like me. My incredible skill of standing still for hours and my greyhound racing speed finally paid off. I snatched that rabbit and it squealed like it was having fun playing with me. Then my neighbor April (I thought that was a month?) who lives in the Apartment House raced to my yard and wrestled the rabbit away from me.

When my mom finally woke up and came outside to get me, April The Tattle Tale told Mom about my morning adventure. I was still frantically trying to dig my way under The Fence when Mom snatched me up, gave me a long stare and saw the evidence of rabbit on my face, marched me back inside and immediately put me in the tub for a bath. She called me a Hot Mess and scrubbed until I was clean and smelled like Burt's Bees Oatmeal Shampoo.

My mom doesn't get mad often but yikes, my Rabbit Adventure did the trick. She built a fence to keep me away from out of the Forbidden Hunting Ground. I did managed to get through the fence a couple more times but she finally secured the area.

I still get to go outside despite the fact that I'm Not To Be Trusted. But seriously, my yard is filled with squirrels, rabbits and chipmunks. What's a pup suppose to do?

Here comes Mom to bring me inside for breakfast. Not as tasty as a rabbit, but my kibble does have a shake or two of Parmesan cheese on top...I bet that would taste good on a rabbit.

19

The Weather

I'm very confused about the weather these days. Some days it's so hot I sit in front of a fan while other days I curl up tight to stay warm. Mom doesn't mind much, unless it interferes with Porch Time or Patio Living.

I've also noticed the sunshine is different. I used to wake up super early which made Mom mad, she's not a morning person. It also gets dark early and I want to go to bed, but Mom is a Night Owl and stays up entirely too late. We are so opposite!

Also The Cat Named Poe was gone for a few days. Mom said he was sick and went to The Vet and it was an expensive event. He stayed in the the Forbidden Bedroom for a few days recovering. I don't know what was wrong with him but he's back to sleeping in my bed. Mom says that's a good sign but it also means that I can't watch The Blue House Across the Street. That cat gets away with everything. Maybe if I stopped peeing on the floor I would get special treatment too.

I have so much to learn. I didn't learn anything in the Puppy Mill. Mom keeps talking about Obedience Lessons. I don't know what that means but if involves treats, pets and snuggles I'm all in! Mom used her Mean Mom Voice at me last night and I shaped up real quick. No snuggles. I'm learning the hard way she says. I looked at her real sad then got a head scratch and we were both happy again. We've both have a lot to learn about Life After The Puppy Mill.

Good Dog...Bad Dog

It's been a week of ups and downs at My New House Across the Street from The Blue House Across the Street.

I'm learning to be a Good Dog! Mom is so proud! I'm learning to share my bed with Fat Cat. He gets the bed all toasty warm before I growl at him and chase him away. Oops. I'm learning to tell Mom when I need to go outside. Last night I pooped outside! I still like to pee inside cuz that grass tickles. Oops. I'm eating all my breakfast and dinner like a Good Dog!

I'm also learning about The Red Collar of Obedience, see Chapter 18. I only wear the Red Collar of Obedience when my brother Ben comes over. When I start to bark at him I hear this crazy beeping sound. I stop barking and turn my head because I'm like "Hey, what was that?". If I keep barking The Collar starts vibrating. Feels kinds good but OK Mom, I get the point. Then I sit down like a Good Dog and let Ben give me head pats. I know I'm in big trouble when that crazy collar beeps and vibrates at the same time. Oops.

The Bad Dog events are the same old same old. Except when Mom thought I was playing with a stick. She thought is was sooo cute. Joke's on Mom though. She saw what it really was (see Chapter 18) and tossed my "stick" over the fence. Oops.

I think this last photo is all that's needed to end this chapter.

21

Chickens, Fences and the Cat Named Poe

The Chickens are roaming freely in the backyard. Mom says it's Fall and they can eat her plants. Less work for her and yard cleanup. I don't know what that means. My yard is perfect! Except for all the extra fences that keep me from escaping and catching rabbits. Oops.

Since The Chickens are roaming freely that means I can take in all the smells in the Happy Hen Hut. I've eaten a bit of their food but that stuff is dry and gross. It's about time Mom let them eat some fresh plants. I tried eating grass and I threw up. Oops.

Guess what I found while snooping in the Happy Hen

Hut? Fresh eggs! Boy they are delicious! And boy did I get in trouble eating them. Oops.

Mom is home all the time now. She has some wierd bandage on her arm. I can't sit on her lap as much and she says "ouch" a lot plus other words that I'm not aloud to say. She seems a little out of it. I hope she gets better soon.

The Cat Named Poe died. We are all very upset. I don't understand any of this. Poe was fun to chase and share my bed with. We spent many hours together staring at The Blue House Across the Street. He made mom very happy. I didn't get a chance to learn from him how to escape without getting yelled at. It's just Me and Fat Cat now. And the Happy Hens. And my brother Ben. Love your family...family is the best.

| 52 |

22

October

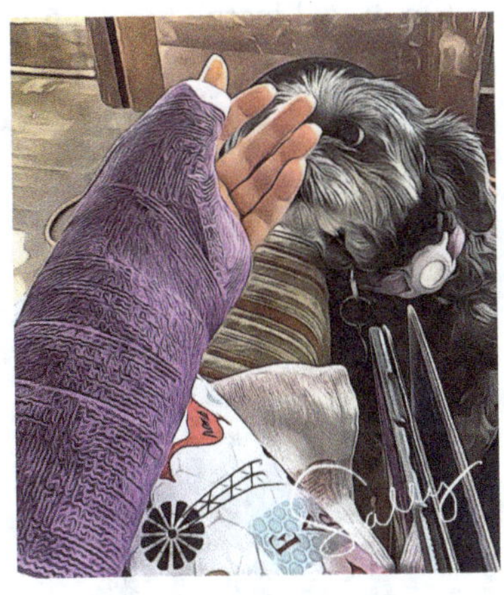

Writing is back at My New House Across the Street from the Blue House Across the Street. Something happened to my mom's hand and she spent lots of time sitting and watching TV and shopping on her iPad. For the whole month! She had many strange bandages on her wrist that were very hard and made getting pets and loves difficult. She also said "OUCH" alot plus a bunch of other words I'm not suppose to say. I heard "surgery" and "thumb" and "arthritis" all the time but since I don't know what any of those words mean I just had to guess that she felt bad. I did my best to be a good dog but there were still a lot of "oops's". Sorry Mom.

In other news it's really cold and Mom puts on my coat every day. She feels bad when I shiver. Our house is really cold too. Something about the boiler and the chimney liner collapsing means no heat until that gets fixed. But I did learn all about the Electric Blanket. What a wonderful invention that is! Fat Cat and I sleep super close to Mom until she budges us out of the way. I learned snuggling is good, budging is not so good.

The cold weather also means no more Front Porch Sitting. I can't see what is going on at the Blue House Across the Street. I miss watching the neighborhood. I sneak out when Mom gets the mail and hop up on my bed. I get scolded because now apparently the Front Porch is part of the Forbidden Zone. I'm so confused. I don't like this change. I think we should move to somewhere warm, but not Florida or Texas. See Chapter 6.

23

Birthday Girl

Guess what? It's my birthday! Happy Birthday! I'm not sure what a birthday is but do know that it is a day of treats and snuggles and whipped cream and a Birthday Biscuit! AND WHIPPED CREAM! Whipped cream is my new favorite thing!

Mom says I am eight years old. I don't feel much different than 7. This is my first birthday celebration. In my old house, the bad puppy mill, there was no celebration with homemade biscuits and whipped cream. I love my new home!

My Brother Ben came over and what a grump he was. No Happy Birthday from him so I did a lot of barking which really made him even grumpier. Then it made Mom mad and we went to take a nap with the Electric Blanket. I love that blanket! So toasty warm.

Now Mom and I are going to snuggle in the blankets and watch TV. I love living in my New House Across the Street from the Blue House Across the Street!

24

Mom Turns 8

I'm still celebrating my 8th Birthday. Mom made lots of those yummy Birthday Biscuits and I get one every day. I've heard rumors about Birthday Week but I never thought it would happen to me! Birthdays are the best.

I've also learned that it's Mom's birthday today! She says we are both the same age now. I'm not so sure about that though. If she's 8 years old why haven't I seen her do zoomies in the back yard? I always beat her to the top of the stairs and she gets out of breath doing simple things. She says it's because she has Idiopathic Subglotic Stenosis. Huh? No excuses when you're 8 Mom.

My Aunt Mary Rose and Uncle Gus took Mom out to dinner last night. I don't know what that means but I did get a sample of what was in her Doggie Bag. I'm so confused. If she brought home a doggie bag why didn't I get to go too? I have so much to learn.

My Brother Ben picked her up for dinner tonight. He said he was cooking Mom New York Strip on The Grill. I love The Grill. See Chapter 10. She brought me home some of the leftovers. Steak is delicious! She had a Cherry Chip Birthday Cake and let me lick the plate. She is a lucky girl.

I didn't get Mom any presents. I don't know how to shop on her iPad. She didn't seem to mind though. She says just having me around is all she needs.

Happy Birthday, Mom!

25

A Year in Review

Mom told me this morning that today is Happy Adoption Day to Me! Does this mean I get more treats?

I can't believe I've lived in My New House Across the Street from The Blue House Across the Street for a whole year! I'm not sure what a that means, but my memories of Missouri are fading, see Chapter 11. I do have bad dreams about it sometimes though. I wake up barking in the middle of the night and scare Mom. She pats me on the head and tells me I'm safe now. Then I settle back down and snuggle against her legs and hog the bed. Oops.

This year I've learned that escaping from my yard is bad, rabbits are delicious and eating grass makes me throw up. Patio Living and Front Porch Sitting are my favorite things in the world. I've mastered the art of walking on a leash and peeing on every scent I smell. I'm a Good Girl when I wear the Red Collar of Obedience when my brother Ben visits. I've learned that I have to share Mom sometimes. I guess that's ok.

I still haven't figured out the whole peeing outside thing. Mom doesn't pee outside so why do I? But life is much better and I don't get yelled at if I go on the pee pad. I hit it most of the time. Oops.

I'm so happy to have a home I can call my own. If you can, please remember to adopt and not shop when looking for a companion. If you rescue a dog from a puppy mill, please be extra kind to your new furry friend. We've been through a lot and don't know how to be a real dog. We have to learn to trust, to love, to play and to obey. Everything is scary! But with lots of love, healthy food and regular vet visits, we will be your loyal companion for as long as we live.

About the Author

Sally is an 8 year old ShiPoo (Shi-Tzu and minature poodle mix) and lived the first years of her life in a puppy mill in Missouri, so there is not a lot of information about her temperment or medical history.

Sally's mom adopted her in December of 2022 from Diamond Dogs Rescue LLC in Madison, WI. After a Facetime interview with the rescue coordinator and references confirmed, Sally moved to her fur-ever home in Dubuque, Iowa to live with her new mom, Colleen.

Sally is thriving in her new home. She has good food to eat, toys to play with and recieves lots of loves from her mom.

www.ingramcontent.com/pod-product-compliance
Lightning Source LLC
Chambersburg PA
CBHW050736150726
48196CB00003B/240